The English Teacher's Handbook

The English Teacher's Handbook

R V White

Nelson Harrap

Thomas Nelson and Sons Ltd
Nelson House, Mayfield Road,
Walton-on-Thames, Surrey
KT12 5PL, UK

51 York Place,
Edinburgh
EH1 3JD, UK

Thomas Nelson (Hong Kong) Ltd
Toppan Building 10/F,
22A Westlands Road,
Quarry Bay, Hong Kong

Distributed in Australia by
Thomas Nelson Australia
480 La Trobe Street,
Melbourne, Victoria 3000
and in Sydney, Brisbane, Adelaide and Perth

First published by George G. Harrap and Co. Ltd
1982 (under ISBN 0-245-53927-1)

Second impression published by Thomas Nelson
and Sons Ltd 1985

Reprinted 1986 (twice)

ISBN 0-17-444184-3

Print No. 04

Cover design by Brooke Calverley
Typeset by Preface Ltd, Salisbury, Wilts.
Printed and bound in Hong Kong

Contents

A Short Guide to English Language Teaching

by RV White

This brief guide to English Language Teaching (ELT) is intended as a simple introduction for teachers who are unfamiliar with the field. It is impossible in such a short space to do justice to the numerous topics which fall within the area of ELT. If you are interested and want to learn more, there are many publications on the subject, as well as a number of journals and magazines. References to some of the most useful of these are given in the Further Reading section. In addition, there are various courses which you can take, ranging in duration from a few days to a complete academic year.

The field of ELT is constantly changing, and there have been some very important changes during recent years. To help give you an overall picture, the traditional or conventional approach to ELT is briefly described below, together with more recent developments. Not everyone accepts or agrees with some of these new trends, while others feel that they are not radical enough. ELT is a field full of controversy, and there is no universally-accepted conventional wisdom.

The descriptions of methodology given here are an attempt to summarize some aspects of current practice. You should not regard them as a guide to the only acceptable method of teaching. You may, however, find them useful additions to your existing teaching skills.

Background

Structuralism in language teaching

The idea that language consists of arrangements of structures is attractive both to language teachers and language learners. After all, the task of learning should be simplified if the students can learn a relatively limited set of structures and if they can substitute a large number of items within the structures. For instance, if they learn a structure such as *a* + noun, the students can make a huge number of substitutions within this structure, or pattern, to produce grammatically correct noun groups like these:

a boy, a pen, a car, a house

The same pattern can be incorporated in a more extensive structure or pattern, thus:

This is a tall boy.
This is a black pen.
This is a new car.
This is a large house.

It is this idea of substitution within a pattern which lies behind the substitution table and the pattern drill, both of which are important components of the structural method. Here is a substitution table based on the above pattern:

This That	is	a	tall black new large	boy. pen. car. house.

Some parts of the table allow more substitutions than others. Some combinations of items from different parts of the table may not be particularly sensible or even polite. For instance, *This is a tall pen* could be used figuratively, but is a statement unlikely to occur in everyday language. To avoid items like this, substitution tables have to be devised so as to prevent meaningless or anomolous choices.

The pattern drill based on the idea of substitution within a structural pattern involves the learners repeating a pattern presented by the teacher, like this:

TEACHER This is a black pen.
CLASS This is a black pen.

1

TEACHER	Car.
CLASS	This is a black car.
TEACHER	Ball.
CLASS	This is a black ball.

Such substitution drills can become more complicated as the teacher selects substitutions at different points in the pattern, like this:

TEACHER	Bill has gone to Paris.
CLASS	Bill has gone to Paris.
TEACHER	New York.
CLASS	Bill has gone to New York.
TEACHER	Flown.
CLASS	Bill has flown to New York.

In addition to substitution within parts of a given pattern, transformation of a pattern is also possible. For instance, the affirmative pattern *This is a* + noun can be transformed into the interrogative pattern *Is this* + *a* + noun? The learners' task is then to transform one pattern into another. The cue is the pattern which is to be transformed:

TEACHER	This is a pen.
CLASS	Is this a pen?
TEACHER	This is a car.
CLASS	Is this a car?

Such transformation drills become more complicated when the tranformation itself is more complex:

TEACHER	John works in an office.
CLASS	Does John work in an office?
TEACHER	Mary works in a shop.
CLASS	Does Mary work in a shop?

The idea behind substitution and transformation drills is appealing because the drills are simple to construct and easy to use in the classroom. There are, however, plenty of traps for both teacher and learners:

TEACHER	He told me to do it.
CLASS	He told me to do it.
TEACHER	Forced.
CLASS	He forced me to do it.
TEACHER	Made.

What are the learners going to do with *made*? Although it belongs in the same general area of meaning as the other verbs, it occurs in a slightly different pattern:

He made me do it.

Based on the other items they have learned, the students are likely to produce the following:

He made me to do it.

Avoiding such problems is one of the issues involved in grading.

Grading

If you decide to adopt a structural approach you are immediately confronted by questions such as:

1   What should I begin with and what should I follow it with? Should I begin with small patterns and build them up into clauses or begin with clauses? Should I begin with the noun group or the verb group? (**sequencing**)

2   What should I teach together? Should I, for example, teach them *tell*, *force* and *require*, or only one of these verbs? Should I teach *make* which has a different structure but a similar meaning to *force*? (**grouping**)

3   How much time should I spend on the various structures? (**staging**)

In fact many of these decisions are taken for you by the author if you are using a structurally-graded textbook. Usually he presents simple structures before more complex forms. And sometimes, because he has chosen to arrange his work according to structural patterns, you may detect signs that he is in trouble – the sentences don't sound quite English, or his story takes on a ludicrous turn. He may move quickly from structure to structure (steep grading) as if bounding up a hill, or he may make the climb more slowly (gentle grading).

Situational teaching

You can, like many textbook writers, choose to teach a foreign language by taking situations the learners are likely to meet and picking out the vocabulary or structures related to them, for example 'At the post office', 'At the railway station'. The difficulty is that the situations may present the learners with a heavy load of vocabulary and too many structures for them to handle.

On the other hand, you can begin with the structures and seek situations that demonstrate them. But some structures are more likely to occur in some situations than others, and you may end up once again with 'textbook

3

English', where you know instinctively something is wrong. So situationally based teaching has its limitations, although it can provide the necessary ingredient of reality for the language which you wish to teach.

Current preoccupations

We use our language system not merely to make up sentences but to use sentences for a purpose. We use language to communicate our feelings, ideas, hopes and fears to other people, and they use their knowledge of the language system to understand our messages. We need to know the vocabulary and structural patterns of the language to do this, of course, but we need something else besides.

In order to appreciate what this 'something else' is, it might be useful to begin by stating what we mean by communication. Briefly, person A sends a message to person B; person B receives the message and reacts to it. Messages are meanings expressed in code, and for our purposes that code is the English language. If the communication is a real one, then B will not already know what A wishes to express. He will have to make an effort to decode the message and then use the code to send back some kind of a message in reply.

Meaning

What kind of meanings can the code carry? We will consider three kinds: referential, notional and functional.

Referential meaning

This kind of meaning is concerned with the labelling of known objects. The word *car* refers to the object car. This labelling function of language is often given a lot of attention in the teaching of vocabulary.

Notional meaning

Look at these two sentences:

(a) Is he going to town?
(b) Is he going to help you?

Is he going has a different notional meaning in each of the two sentences. In (a) it conveys the abstract idea, or notion, of movement to a place. In (b) it carries the idea of someone's intentions about the future. In other words, it expresses the notion of futurity.

Here are some more sentences:

Tom is taller than Bill.
Bill is shorter than Henry.
Henry is the tallest.

5

All these sentences express the notion or concept of comparison. Concepts or notions like these are conveyed in everything we say or write, and most things we say express more than one notion.

Functional meaning

We can illustrate the third type of meaning with the following dialogue:

A Excuse me. How can I get to the car park from here?
B Just go up this corridor, turn left and then go down the stairs.
A Thanks.

Each speaker here has used language for several different purposes. Speaker A begins by attracting attention (*Excuse me*), and continues by requesting direction (*How can I get . . .*). Speaker B responds by directing Speaker A to the place concerned. Finally, Speaker A thanks Speaker B. Attracting attention, requesting, directing and thanking are all examples of language functions. Functional meaning is concerned with expressing our intentions. The names of functions are usually either verbs, such as *ask, invite, instruct, report, persuade*, or verb-based nouns, such as *asking, inviting, instructing, reporting, persuading*.

The function of a sentence changes with context. This means that the same form of words can have a different function, depending on the situation and the other sentences surrounding it. Here are two examples:

(a) A I think we've got everything.
    B What about the camera?
    A It's in the case.

(b) A I think we've got everything.
    B What about the camera?
    A We'd better take it with us.

In (a) B's question is understood to be a request for information. In other words, the function of B's utterance is to ask where something is. In (b) the same words have a quite different function. Here they are used to make a suggestion. So one utterance can perform many different functions, depending on the context. Similarly, there are many different ways of expressing one and the same function.

Appropriateness

At the beginning of this section, we said that you need to know more than the vocabulary and structures of the language in order to use language for a purpose. What we need to know is, firstly, how to express our intentions,

6

and secondly, when to use the various expressions appropriately. In the dialogue above where speaker A asks for directions, we could have begun like this:

A   Hi, you. Tell me how to get to the car park from here.

Most people would consider this to be rather rude. On the other hand, the following would be considered excessively polite:

A   Excuse me, kind sir. I wonder if you would be so kind as to direct me to the car park from here.

Students have to learn when, and when not, to use expressions like those given above. They also have to learn when to use different levels of politeness or formality. Recognizing and using different ways of expressing language functions are among the concerns of current language teaching.

Information gap

There is another preoccupation which is connected with the communication of messages as described above. Communication takes place when the receiver doesn't already know the information in the sender's message. In other words, there is an information gap, which is filled by the message. In the following classroom exchange, there is no information gap:

TEACHER   John went to town. Did John go to town?
CLASS   Yes, he did.

In this exchange, both the sender (the teacher) and the receiver (the class) know the information (that John went to town). The question is not a real question. The answer is not a real answer. There is no information gap and there is no real communication.

Improvisation

Another important feature of communication is improvisation. We have to make and interpret messages as we speak and listen, without prior preparation or rehearsal. Even in a simple conversational exchange there is an element of the unexpected and unpredictable. This means that both speakers have to be ready to react in any one of several ways. Both speakers have to be able to improvise.

A fluent speaker is able to improvise with little difficulty. The learner of English finds it more difficult. Yet when he steps out of the classroom and tries to use English in the real world, he will have to improvise all the time.

Unfortunately, students are not always given much practice in improvising. Another current preoccupation in the language classroom is providing opportunities for improvising. This can be done by setting up communicative tasks in which each student cannot predict what his partner will say. His own response will therefore have to be made up on the spot, and he will have to decide how to react, and what to say. In responding, he will be forced to exploit the language he knows in the most effective way.

Such improvisation can and should involve ingenuity on the part of the student. For instance, if the student either doesn't know or can't remember a needed vocabulary item, he can use known or remembered language instead. For example if the student can't remember the word *square*, then he could substitute a phrase like *a thing with four equal sides*. We improvise in this way in our native language when we don't have the necessary word to hand, and it is one of the improvisatory skills which we now feel should be encouraged when learning to use English as a foreign or second language.

Communication in the classroom

As we have seen, there is currently much interest in setting up communication situations in the classroom so that students can practise and improvise using language to communicate real messages. This usually involves giving pairs of students complementary sets of information. In order to complete the gaps in their information, they have to communicate real messages to each other. For example, you can give student A an incomplete train timetable, while student B has the completed version. Student A then has to ask student B for the train times in order to complete the gaps in his information.

This is a simple example of a communicative activity in the classroom. There are many other communicative activities ranging from simple ones, such as the train timetable exercise, to much more complex ones involving several students, and more complicated tasks and messages. What most of these activities have in common is the principle of information gap as well as the need for students to improvise.

Some communication activities are described in the section on speaking. There are also many published materials containing the basis for communication activities. There are published sets of role- or cue-cards, language games, and simulations. In fact, it is difficult to set up pair-work communicative activities within the pages of a textbook, as it is often important that each student only has access to his own cue or prompt and not to that of his partner as well. Publishers are now producing packs of materials so that the information or the prompts needed for the activities can be separately distributed between pairs or among members of a group.

Using authentic materials

The current interest in using language in realistic ways has led to the increased use of authentic materials in language teaching. Authentic materials are pieces of language, either spoken or written, which were originally messages produced for communication in a non-teaching situation. Such messages are genuine pieces of communication designed for native speakers, so they are not structurally graded. Nor are they organized in order to demonstrate a language teaching point. Traditionally, such authentic materials have been thought of as 'advanced', for use only with students who already know quite a lot of the language.

It is now felt that students at all levels can benefit from being exposed to authentic materials. Such materials are linguistically rich and they give students the opportunity to extend their experience of English. Students who are not exposed to authentic language may have a nasty shock when they meet real English outside the classroom. Experience of authentic language in the classroom can help reduce this shock, and prepare learners to cope with the range, speed and variety of the authentic language they will meet. Authentic material is, moreover, potentially more interesting than texts which have been specially contrived for language teaching purposes. Even cleverly contrived texts are never entirely natural. They distort the language by presenting structures and functions in ways which may not be authentic, thus giving the students a false idea of how the language is used.

There are, however, some problems with using authentic texts. To begin with, once you use an authentic text as a piece of teaching material, it ceases to be authentic. The student is now the receiver of the message, whereas originally the receiver was someone who was a user, not a learner, of English. The relationship of the student to an authentic text is quite different, therefore, from the relationship of an authentic receiver.

Let us take an example. The authentic reader of a newspaper is reading about news which is current. There may be a lot of coverage of one particular event in the media, and this event may be a topic of everyday conversation. The newspaper reader may read the latest news report about this event with a lot of background knowledge. The new report will fit into this existing context. The news is also current – perhaps the event happened the day before. The language learner confronted with an authentic text doesn't have any of this background; nor is the news current. So the student reading a newspaper report is tackling it from a very different viewpoint from that of the original audience. Using authentic texts may thus involve providing a lot of background information – in other words, establishing the context.

Another problem – and one which every teacher will be aware of – is the level of language difficulty found in authentic texts. Teachers often avoid using authentic material because the language will tend to be well outside the range of their students' English. This need not be a problem, though, because the difficulty for the students will not be so much in the language – it will be in the things you ask them to do with the text. If the language is difficult, then you should ask them to perform very simple tasks with the text. If the language is easy, then ask them to do something more difficult.

Take the example of a newspaper report about an accident. Such reports invariably include details about the victims – names, ages, occupations, the place where the accident took place, the effects of the accident – injuries, damage, and some information on the condition of the victims. Students don't need much English in order to pick out the gist of the report. Names and numbers are easily identified, so the students can find out who was involved and where and when the accident took place. They will also be able to find out whether the accident involved cars, trains, planes or boats, or a combination of these, since all these things should be within the vocabulary presented in the first year of most English courses. So, using a very little language, the students can discover quite a lot from a so-called 'advanced' authentic text. If you used the same text with more advanced students you could demand more detailed comprehension.

Finally, we need to distinguish between authentic texts and authentic tasks. Using authentic materials doesn't make the language activities themselves any more authentic. Nothing that we do in the classroom can be truly authentic if we compare the teaching situation with the real world. Even so, we may wish to reproduce some of the features of the real world in the classroom as an aid to motivation and learning. To do this, we should always think about the reality of the tasks and activities that we set our students to do.

Let us return to our example from a newspaper – the report of an accident. A non-authentic task would be to analyse the text in great detail. Such reports are not usually written to be studied and analysed. For instance, if there was an accident involving half a dozen cars, detailed information about the vehicles would be less important than the fact that so many cars were involved. It would be a non-authentic task to ask the students to identify and recall highly specific details from a report of this kind.

So when you are using authentic materials you need to consider the authenticity of the task as well. Ask yourself such questions as 'Why do I read or listen to such texts?' and 'What do I use such texts for?' and 'What do I do when I read or listen to such material?' If you find that you are getting your students to perform unreal tasks and activities with authentic material, ask yourself if they are really useful. Try to devise more authentic tasks.

Focus on the learner

Another current preoccupation is concerned with the learner and learning. This preoccupation centres on three aspects of the learner: the errors which the learner makes, the correction of those errors and the learner's language learning needs.

Errors

Traditionally, teachers have tended to think of learners' errors as bad. In structurally-based teaching the teacher tried to prevent the learner from producing errors at all. It was felt that if the learner made errors, they would become part of his language habits. More recent theories on language and language learning take a different view. Now it is felt that making errors is a natural part of learning a language. Some researchers have found striking similarities between the errors made by children learning their native language and foreign speakers learning the same language. Such errors are called 'developmental errors' and they show that the student is using his intuitive language learning abilities to learn the new language system. Some people believe that unless the learner is allowed to make such developmental errors, his learning of the foreign language will be less efficient.

Learners also make other errors which can be caused by the way the new language is presented. We noted earlier that a student can make an error by analogy if first given the pattern, *He told me to do it*. When the learner is given the verb *make* he is likely to use it in the same pattern, *He made me to do it*. This is a perfectly natural error and it is caused not by a deficiency in the learner, but by faulty organization of material by the teacher or textbook writer.

There are other errors which can be caused by faulty presentation. Here is a typical example:

TEACHER   Did John go to town?
STUDENT   Yes, he go to town.

It is obvious that the learner has focused on the simple verb form and the meaning of the verb, rather than on the complicated rules involved in forming the past tense affirmative when replying to a past tense question. It is quite common for teachers to be very critical of students who make such 'basic' mistakes, and when the students are reminded of the grammatical rule, they can often recognize their mistake. What the teacher has to remember is that he has helped the student to make the mistake by using the question pattern in which the base form of the verb occurs straight after the subject. A student who is struggling to remember the correct past tense form of *go* is sure to be confused, and so will make an elementary error.

The emphasis on grammatical accuracy has now given way to greater interest in fluency. It is possible to speak a foreign language with considerable fluency, and yet to make errors of grammar, vocabulary and accent when compared with a native speaker. Teachers are now told to be more tolerant of errors, particularly when they are trying to encourage learners to communicate. The insensitive correction of errors during a communicative activity can inhibit the learner and destroy the whole point of the exercise.

Error correction

Although there is a more tolerant attitude towards student errors now, this does not mean that errors are encouraged. The teacher should still help the students to correct errors. The question is, how should he do this? One answer is that the teacher should correct all errors as they occur. It has been said that teacher correction of errors is often muddled, inconsistent and ineffective, and there is some evidence that this is indeed so. Another answer is that the teacher should encourage the students to notice their own errors and to correct themselves. This argument implies that the only effective form of error correction is that which involves the student rather than the teacher. After all, the student cannot always depend on having a teacher at his side to correct errors.

A third answer would be a compromise between these two views. There is no point in trying to correct any and all errors as they occur in class. There should instead be a focus on particular language items. Decide which errors you are going to deal with and ignore the others for the time being. If you and your students know which errors you are concentrating on, you can work together on the same problem. If you are focusing on a structural error, for example, you shouldn't become sidetracked by pronunciation problems as well. If you do, you may find that you spend a large part of your lesson dealing with the wrong errors. You also need to give more and more responsibility to the students for identifying and correcting their own errors. This is particularly true of written work and this is discussed in the section on the teaching of writing.

You may find that unexpected errors occur, or that a certain type of error proves to be widespread. Make a note of these errors and devote some time to dealing with them in future lessons. In fact, you may well find that you have to spend some time on correcting persistent errors – perhaps ten minutes each lesson for several weeks, if you see your class only two or three times a week. Very few errors can be corrected after only one remedial lesson, so you must expect to keep coming back to the same problems. This is another good reason for concentrating on a few important errors rather than trying to deal with everything at once. A good rule to follow is: Don't dissipate – concentrate!

The learner's needs

A lot of attention has been given recently to identifying the needs of the learner. By 'needs' we generally mean the reasons why a given student has to learn English. For some groups of students, the needs are easily identified. If, for instance, you are going to teach a businessman who is going to come and live and work in Britain for a period of time, you can identify his language learning needs under such headings as Social, Occupational, Recreational, Cultural, and so on. Or, if you are going to teach airline cabin crews, you can predict their language learning needs even more easily, because they will be using English in very limited circumstances with a restricted range of functions, topics, and so on.

The picture is not so clear, though, if you are teaching secondary school pupils. Probably only a few of them will have any real need to learn English. Possibly none of them will ever have a use for it once they have left school. Possibly some of them may go on to further education in which a knowledge of English is essential. But we cannot always predict what our students will do once they leave school. So finding out their language learning needs can be very difficult.

Another problem arises with any group of learners. Teachers, employers and people in authority may decide what the students need. But it is the students themselves who say what they want. There is always a difference between needs and wants. If there is a very big difference, teaching the students will be rather difficult, the more so if you don't find out what their wants are. Why do they want to learn English? What are they interested in? When and with whom do they want to use English? Do they want to learn to speak English? Or would they prefer to read and write it? These are the kinds of questions which will help to find what the students' wants are. Once you know their wants, you can try to organize some of your teaching to satisfy them. This should help raise the students' motivation, and will help to achieve their language learning needs as well.

Current practice: the four skills

It has long been conventional to think of language teaching in terms of the so-called four skills: listening, speaking, reading and writing. The method of language teaching known as audiolingualism regarded speech as primary, and a great deal of emphasis was placed on speaking practice, with reading and writing being introduced later largely to reinforce language which had already been practised through speech. Investigations into the characteristics of spoken and written language have shown that speaking is not just a debased or simplified form of writing and that writing is not just an attempt to put spoken language on paper. Consequently, we no longer treat one skill as a reflection of another. Each skill tends to be treated in its own right. The amount of time given to each skill will depend on the needs and wants of the learner as specified in the syllabus. There is little sense, for instance, in spending hours practising the spoken language if all the students need to learn is to read English.

As variety is also important in the language classroom, all four skills will have their place. Even the student who only needs to read English will benefit from some practice in listening, speaking and writing. Some people, moreover, do seem to be better at learning by listening and speaking while others are better at learning by reading and writing. So using all four skills is important in order to give all students a chance to use their abilities as best they can.

Finally, integration of skills is a feature of current practice. This means that any one lesson may exercise all four skills, for instance with information that is provided in a listening comprehension exercise being used for spoken or written practice later in the same lesson. Similarly, reading comprehension may provide the basis for spoken discussion which will recycle information obtained in the reading phase of the lesson.

Listening

There is some evidence that giving beginners lots of listening practice before asking them to speak is more beneficial than getting them to speak from the very first stage. Listening alone is not enough, as the students' listening needs to be directed in order to be beneficial.

So, at the earliest stage of learning, the students need to be given help in identifying where sentences, phrases and words begin and end. In other words, they need help in recognizing some of the structures of the language. You can help them to do this by isolating words from their sentence context and then putting them back into phrases or sentences again. If you are using real objects or pictures, students can be asked to point to or identify the object or illustration referred to in an utterance. Contrastive differences between sounds, for example the vowel sounds in *pin* and *pen*, can be linked to choices which students have to make when presented with such requests as *Give me a pin* or *Give me a pen*.

Once you have introduced the students to writing, you can give some simple dictation exercises. Traditionally, dictation tended to be word-by-word writing down from speech. Although such dictation has its place, there is a need for much more variety. For instance, focused dictation can involve writing down only items which have been selected in advance by the teacher. So if you want to focus on the unstressed indefinite article, *a/an*, you could give the students a list of nouns as they appear in a dictation passage. The students will be instructed to write in *a* or *an* before each noun as it occurs as you read the passage with normal unstressed articulation of the articles. Alternatively, you might want to focus on the plural form of a given group of nouns. The students are given a list of the nouns in the non-plural form, and they have to add the plural ending only to those which occur in the plural in the dictation passage. Again, a normal unstressed reading should be given so as to avoid exaggerating the focused feature.

Similar focusing can be done with prepositions, which are often unstressed and are difficult to perceive. You can provide a written version of the dictation in which the prepositions have been left out. The students have to write the correct preposition in the blank space as they listen to the dictation. Alternatively, they could be asked to add the prepositions before listening. The dictation then gives them an opportunity to check their completions.

A more difficult version of this exercise involves a variation on the cloze technique. Every so often a word is deleted from a text – often every seventh word. The students first attempt to complete the gaps. Then the teacher reads the text. The students listen, but they don't follow the written text, as this would make the exercise too easy. After hearing the dictation, they return to the text and check their version. Other combinations of reading and listening can be used, and in all cases the students should be placed in the position of having to make an effort to identify and write down the language items concerned.

Finally, focused dictations which emphasize sequence or order can be used. For instance, if you are dealing with the past tense for telling stories, you can give the pupils a muddled list of the past tense verbs which occur in the dictation text. Their task is to number the verbs in sequence as they appear in the story when it is read aloud. The correctly numbered verb sequence can then be used to re-tell the story. Note, though, that there is a limit to the number of verbs which you can handle in this way – about ten or twelve is the maximum. Sequence is also important in the noun-group in

English, and you can give your students a number of noun-groups in which the words are in muddled order, for example *blue the car large*. As the students listen to the dictation, they number the words in the correct order. Subsequently, they write out the noun-groups with the words in the correct order, possibly as part of a sentence-completion exercise.

All of the above suggestions are ways of helping learners to cope with word boundaries, word order and word form (for example, singular and plural nouns). The focus is on structure rather than meaning or function. If we move to the comprehension of spoken messages, the focus shifts from words or phrases to longer stretches of speech. There is, currently, a great deal of interest in using authentic spoken language, such as recordings of impromptu and unscripted conversations. Some publishers have made such material available in easily-usable form. (See above for a discussion of authentic materials.)

The availability of the cassette recorder has led to the widespread use of pre-recorded authentic material, even for the individual student working alone. At the same time our increased understanding of the characteristics of spoken language has made us aware of the importance of using real spoken language for listening comprehension, and not written language read aloud by the teacher. Reading aloud a comprehension passage from a textbook is not a good basis for training listening comprehension. Fortunately, there are many other ways of dealing with listening comprehension, and most published listening materials give explicit and helpful suggestions. What follows is a general set of procedures which you can adapt and vary as you wish.

Stage one   It is a good idea to lead in to the listening phase of the lesson by arousing student interest or motivation. Ask them to make some guesses about the content of the recording they are about to hear. Tell them, for instance, it is a conversation between two people who haven't seen each other for a long time. Ask the class what sort of things they might talk about. These guesses can be listed on the blackboard.

Stage two   The recording should be played straight through, with the students listening in order to get an overall idea of what the recording is about. If you have made a blackboard list of possible content, the students can listen to see how many of their suggested topics are actually covered in the recording. After the first hearing, you and the class review the black-board list, noting which topics were covered and adding any which weren't on the list. Elicit these topics from the students.

Stage three   Play the recording again, but this time direct the students to listen for particular pieces of information. Don't ask them for too many details, as it is very difficult to identify and recall a lot of information when we listen, even in our native language. At an elementary level, you may ask them to listen for very simple pieces of information, such as dates, times or names. Or you might ask them to identify one particular piece of information from a lot of similar information, for example in a weather forecast. When we listen to highly detailed texts, such as weather forecasts, we tend to take in only information of particular interest to ourselves, such as the predictions for the region where we live.

Stage four   Give out a previously prepared worksheet for students to complete. This may be done either during the second or third hearing, depending on the length, difficulty and complexity of the material and tasks. If the worksheet is fairly complicated, it will be difficult for the students to listen and complete it simultaneously. In this case, it may be better to ask them to complete the worksheet after a second hearing. It may also be better to get them to complete the worksheet in pairs or small groups, so that they can discuss and compare their information.

Stage five   Play the recording a final time so that the students can check their completion of the worksheet. This final hearing should, like the previous ones, be uninterrupted. It isn't usually a good idea to keep stopping and starting the tape, as this breaks up the material and reduces the students' opportunity to follow a continuous piece of material. They won't be able to stop and start anything they are listening to outside the classroom.

There are variations on these procedures. You may wish to help develop your students' powers of prediction by stopping the tape at several points and asking them to suggest what the speaker might say next. This doesn't mean that they have to predict the exact words, but rather the kind of thing, or the function, which the speaker might utter. Such an exploded, or broken up, hearing of the tape should always precede a global, or uninterrupted hearing. If you do break a recording into smaller sections, you should provide a global hearing at some point in the lesson so that the students do hear all of it in order to see how the various shorter sections fit together.

You may also want to focus on particular language functions, structures or expressions in the material. Detailed focusing is best left until the students have listened to the tape several times for content. This would mean adding a sixth stage during which the students' attention is turned to language rather than meaning. This fits in with the idea of moving from the global to the specific, of analysing the whole into smaller pieces rather than trying to put together a number of small pieces to make up a larger whole.

To summarize, listening comprehension work should exploit realistic, but not necessarily authentic, spoken material. It should not be written material read aloud. Undirected and unmotivated listening tends to be inefficient and ineffective. Students need to know why they are listening and what to listen for. To help provide motivation, use the information from the listening stage for another activity, such as a discussion, a composition or the completion of a task which cannot be performed without having done the listening comprehension exercise first.

Speaking

Speaking involves being able to use the sound system of English. In order to do this, the student needs to have a good model. Ideally, this would be a native speaker of English. Fortunately, in the absence of a native speaker in the classroom, we now have ready access to recordings of native English speakers, and there are published materials which are intended to help the student learn some of the basic sounds and tunes of English as spoken by native speakers.

To help make your students sensitive to the differences between their own language and English, you can ask them to try speaking their own language with an English accent. This is usually an amusing activity, and it helps to highlight some of the differences between the native language sound system and that of English. Next, you can use some minimal pair sound exercises already referred to in the previous section (page 15). In these exercises you produce pairs of words which differ in only one sound, and students have to say whether the words are the same or different, for example *live* and *leave*, and *pin* and *bin*. Choose only those sounds where there is likely to be some difficulty because the native language lacks the contrast which is present in English. If the contrast exists in the native language, there is no point in dealing with it.

Follow up discrimination exercises with productive practice by the students. Sometimes it may be necessary to provide an explanation of how the sound is articulated or produced in order to help the students produce it themselves. For instance, Spanish has a *v* sound which is produced with the upper lip in a position very similar to that of *b* in English, whereas English *v* is produced with the upper teeth resting briefly on the lower lip. An explanation and demonstration of this difference would be necessary when teaching Spanish speaking students how to produce a *v* in English.

Minimal pair exercises deal only with individual elements of sound. Intonation, or the tune and rhythm of English, is a more difficult area for many learners. Several techniques can be used to help. Firstly, familiarize students with the basic tunes and secondly, help them reproduce them in their own speech. One technique is to 'sing' the tune using *la-la-la*, instead of words, as the sound units. Such singing can be accompanied by hand gestures to illustrate the rise and fall in pitch and the rhythm. The intonation contour can be drawn on the blackboard, using a line which rises and falls according to the characteristics of the tune. This contour can be superimposed on the words of the utterance, also written on the blackboard.

Stress can be indicated by short vertical lines above the stressed word or syllable in an utterance. Harrap's *Easy English Dictionary*, for example, uses this convention to indicate stress, so it is useful to teach students the significance of the marking. To develop students' sensitivity to stress, give some short dictation exercises in which they have to mark stress in this way.

Avoid using a very complicated set of markings to show intonation. If the system of markings requires a great deal of effort to learn, students will quickly become discouraged. The system of markings should act as an aid but not an end in itself. Once it becomes an end in itself, students are simply learning about intonation rather than using correct and appropriate intonation in their own speech. The same applies to training your students in phonetic transcription as a way of teaching the sounds of English. Any aid such as this, which adds to the learning burden rather than taking away from it, will be treated with suspicion by the students and is unlikely to be very effective.

Ideally, the teaching of intonation will go hand in hand with the teaching of language functions . Unfortunately, very little work has so far been done on the link between intonation and function and there is little published material which shows how function, attitude and appropriateness are associated with differences in intonation. At a very simple level, a rising intonation in English is associated with the function of asking for information, or questioning. Speakers of some languages tend to use a rising intonation in English when making statements. This can have unfortunate results when communicating with native English speakers. To try to overcome this problem, there is a need to link the teaching of intonation and the functional use of language.

A fundamental problem which has to be dealt with in the spoken English class is simply encouraging students to speak. This may be achieved by working through a number of stages, from complete language control by the teacher to a large degree of freedom by the students.

Stage one   Ask students to repeat a scripted dialogue, usually one which appears in the textbook. You can present the dialogue to the class by playing a recording of it or by taking both parts yourself. Then ask one of the students to take part B while you take part A. Next ask another student to take part A, and have the two students repeat the dialogue for the rest of the the class. Finally, put the class into A and B pairs, and get them to take turns at reading both parts of the dialogue.

Stage two   This involves making substitutions within the basic framework of the original dialogue. The textbook may suggest substitutions, or you can add some yourself, or you can ask the students to suggest some. For instance, a dialogue concerned with the function of making suggestions might permit substitutions in the form of the suggestion (for example *How about going...?, What about going...?, Let's go...*) as well as in the content of the suggestion (*to the cinema, to a disco, to a play, to a pop concert* and so on). It may also allow for substitutions in the functions themselves so that, for instance, a suggestion could be followed either by an agreement (*Yes, that's a good idea*) or by a refusal, a reason and a counter suggestion (*No, it's too crowded. What about going to a concert?*). Once the substitutions have been sorted out and one or two demonstrations given, following the procedure described in the first stage of the lesson, students can do some more pair practice, this time using the substitutions.

Stage three Students are now given more freedom over language and the form of the dialogue. Instead of giving the students their lines, as in a play script, they can be given cues or prompts which tell them the function but not the actual language which they should perform. In order to make the dialogue more like real life, the cues should be given on separate cards so that student A cannot see student B's cues and vice versa. (See the principle of information gap discussed on page 7). The cues might look like this:

Student A	*Student B*
Greet B.	Greet A.
Ask B what he/she is doing tonight.	
Suggest that you go to a disco.	Say you are free.
	Refuse. Give a reason. Make another suggestion.
Agree. Arrange a time.	
	Arrange a time.

What the students have to decide on is, firstly, the form of the utterances and secondly, the precise content. To do this they make use of the language which they have practised in earlier stages.

Stage four This could provide even more choice for each student by giving them a role to play. In this case, the information might be provided in the following form. (Again, each student sees only his own role-card.)

Student A

You like dancing and going to discos. Suggest to your partner that you go out this evening. Try to persuade him/her to go where you prefer.

Student B

You don't like dancing and going to discos. You prefer going to the cinema or to a concert. Try to persuade your partner to go where you prefer.

These examples are instances of communicative activities. Such activities are useful as a way of providing students at all levels with opportunities to communicate without having to rely on the teacher. For instance, you can use 'find or describe the difference' activities at every level from beginners to advanced. In this type of activity, each partner in the pair is supplied with identical pictures which differ in a number of points, such as the presence or absence of certain features, the number of a given item, location, colour, and so on. Each partner, describes and/or questions in order to reveal or discover the differences between the two pictures. A variant on the same theme is 'describe and arrange' or 'describe and draw' in which one partner describes an arrangement of figures or a picture while the partner either arranges the same components (for example, geometrical figures, cuisinnaire rods) or tries to draw the picture as described by his partner.

A third type of communicative activity involves the solving of a problem through discussion. The students are given a problem to solve together. They are given some information which they can use to reach a solution. The information can be presented as part of a listening or reading comprehension in which the students complete a worksheet. The completed worksheet then becomes the source for the information they need in their discussion. For instance, the problem could be trying to arrange an outing or a meeting. The information could take the form of diary entries for the people involved. The discussion will involve suggesting alternative days and times and finally reaching an agreement on a time which suits everyone best.

Alternatively, the problem could involve a puzzle of a type such as the following:

A man is standing by a bend in a river. He wishes to cross the river, but he has only two planks of wood. He can't use them as a raft or a boat, and the two planks aren't long enough to form a bridge. Decide how he can use the pieces of wood to get across the river without getting his feet wet.

In the teaching of speaking skills, there is a progression from exercises which focus on sounds to activities which provide the student with choice and freedom for practising communication. Each type of exercise has its place. Before you ask your students to communicate, you will generally have to give them some models of language and some controlled practice. The communicative activities may occupy a relatively short period at the end of a lesson. They are important, though, because they give students an opportunity of using what they have learnt. They also put the students into a position where they have to improvise, thus reproducing a feature of real-life language use outside the classroom. (See the earlier discussion on improvisation in the section on current preoccupations.)

Reading

There are two separate stages involved in reading. There is the initial stage of decoding, that is recognizing the relationship between the print on the page and the sounds of the language. This is the first step in learning to read. Traditionally, students have read aloud to demonstrate their ability to connect printed symbol and spoken sound.

The second stage is that of comprehension. It is possible to read aloud a piece of writing in a foreign language without understanding a word of it. Comprehension involves more than simply decoding. It involves recognizing the significance of the message, understanding the intentions of the writer, and going beyond what is written to guess at hidden, unstated or implied meanings.

In the early stages of learning to read, it may be helpful for the teacher to read the passage aloud to the class while the pupils follow the text in their books. The teacher will provide a better model than any of the pupils can give if they read aloud, but the act of reading aloud does no more than help the students to see the relationship between print and sound. Because written language is different from spoken language, it isn't a satisfactory form of listening comprehension, and you shouldn't expect pupils to attend to such a reading as if it were a piece of ordinary spoken language.

Once students have gone beyond the first stage of decoding printed messages, they will be ready to understand the message itself. Understanding messages depends on a number of things – our knowledge of the world, our reasons for reading and our attitudes and beliefs. The teacher's job is to help create reasons for wanting to read something, and to help organize the students' thinking so that what they read fits into an existing mental framework.

This can be done in several ways. For instance, if you are going to deal with a non-fiction text which provides a lot of information on a given topic, you can ask the class to say what they already know about the topic. Volunteering such information can become quite animated and students may dispute certain points. You can then list points on the board under such headings as 'What we know', 'What we don't know' or 'Sure' and 'Uncertain'. Having stimulated class interest, you can then issue the reading text, or tell the class to turn to the appropriate page in their textbook, and instruct them to read it in order to confirm or contradict the points which are listed on the board.

This type of reading exercise is less appropriate when dealing with narrative or fiction. In the case of narrative and stories, the sequence of events or actions will usually be important. A preparatory stage can involve giving the students a set of pictures or a set of sentences which are in random or muddled order. The students' task is to put the pictures or sentences into logical order. They then read the text in order to verify the narrative sequence which they have worked out. An alternative is to give out the muddled pictures or sentences and tell the class to read the text. They then put the illustrations or sentences into correct order following the events in the story.

A third type of text requires an entirely different technique. Texts which describe arrangements of things or the organization of actions can be linked to diagrams or pictures. For instance, a text which directs the reader in how to get from one place to another can be used with a map. The students' task will be to fill in a route on the map according to the directions in the text. Alternatively, the text might describe a place or object. In this case, the students could label a picture of the place or object. Finally, the text might describe a process or procedure. In this case, the student could label a diagrammatic summary of the process.

Activities involving drawing, labelling or completing a diagram or visual of some sort are examples of information transfer. In other words, information presented in a written text is transferred to a visual form. Such information transfer activities are currently very popular, though they don't necessarily involve drawing or labelling. For example, the students can be given a text and an illustration. They are told that there are a number of mistakes, either in the text or in the illustration. If the text is correct, there will be errors in the illustration and vice versa. The students' task is to identify the errors and make appropriate corrections to the text or the picture.

In addition to such activities, there are the more traditional true/false and multiple choice comprehension exercises. In the former, the students are given a number of statements about the text which are either true or false, according to the information in the passage. The students read the text and then answer the true/false items. Multiple choice items consist of a statement with a number of possible conclusions. Usually three choices are provided. The student has to choose the correct conclusion according to the information in the passage.

Such activities can be criticized as being concerned with testing the students' comprehension without actually teaching them how to read a text effectively. This is certainly the case if the individual student is expected to complete the items as an individual activity. There is, however, no need always to handle reading as a solo activity. If small groups of three or four students are given multiple choice items to work on, they can discuss among themselves which alternative they would choose and why they would reject the others. In this way, they can engage in useful discussion about the text and the meanings which the writer intended to convey.

Fruitful discussion and purposeful reading can also be promoted when the reading comprehension exercise is part of a set of activities with a final product or solution. For instance, the students might be given a task which involves planning or choosing something. The first reading task will involve reading a text in which someone's requirements are described. The second task will consist of reading several texts in order to discover the best or most appropriate choice for these requirements. The actual task might be concerned with purchasing a piece of equipment for a school. The texts would therefore consist of descriptions of possible pieces of equipment, and the students would identify the particular piece which most closely matched the requirements that had been specified.

The reading lesson could take one of several forms. The simplest type of lesson would involve four stages.

Stage one   Arouse the students' interest and motivation by linking the topic of the text to their own experience or existing knowledge.

Stage two   Give them points to search for in the reading text, or ask the students themselves to suggest such points.

Stage three   After the students have read the text and found the specified information, encourage discussion of their answers and deal with alternative interpretations. Dealing with wrong answers can be just as important as looking at correct ones.

Stage four   It may be useful and productive if the students use the information they have gathered or the answers they have obtained for a further task, such as a piece of writing. This means that the reading comprehension exercise doesn't end with reading the text. Instead, the information is used for another purpose, thus giving further point to the reading.

24

In addition to classroom reading and reading comprehension exercises, you should encourage your students to read as much as possible outside of class. The best way to do this is to have a library of graded or simplified readers, of which there is an extensive selection from the major ELT publishers. It is a good idea to keep a record of students' reading, so that you can make sure that all students complete at least one reader a term. You may also find it useful to ask students to tell you a little bit about what they are reading. Over a term you can spend a few minutes discussing with each student their current reader, even in a large class. But remember that out of class reading should be enjoyable, so don't expect your students to read material that is too difficult, and don't make them feel that they are being tested on what they read.

Writing

As a means of communication, writing differs from speaking in several important ways. Firstly, writing is permanent, speaking is not. Secondly, we can correct what we write before it is received by the reader. Corrections when we speak tend to take place after we have already made an error which our audience has received. Thirdly, we usually write for a receiver who is physically absent from us, whereas most speaking that we do is for an audience which is actually present as we speak. Fourthly, the physical distance between writer and reader means that the reader can't easily ask the writer to explain something unclear or ambiguous. In face-to-face speech, such feedback from listener to speaker is instantaneous. So the writer has to be very careful to ensure that his written message is complete in itself. He shouldn't make any assumptions about shared knowledge between himself and his audience. Nor should the writer leave any room for misunderstandings through unclear expression or faulty organization of his text.

Writing exercises are of two types – those which consolidate language already presented and practised orally, and those which develop the skills of communicating in writing.

Most textbooks contain plenty of examples of the first type, although such exercises are limited in what they can achieve. They may require the student to practise writing a number of unrelated sentences, and although this is perfectly acceptable as a practice activity, it must be remembered that we hardly ever actually write only one sentence at a time. A written message usually consists of a number of interrelated sentences.

Another limitation of such exercises is that they test students instead of teaching them. Typically, students are given a rule or an example, and then have to produce a number of other sentences in which the rule is applied. Sometimes this can result in the production of complicated sentences which would hardly ever actually be written. The students are simply practising instances of classroom or textbook language.

A third limitation is giving students instructions such as 'Write these sentences with the verbs in brackets in the correct tense.' The students are then given a series of sentences with the infinitive form of the verb as a prompt. They have to convert these infinitives into the correct tense, which can be a confusing and difficult task with the infinitive acting as a distractor. Such exercises tend to test the students before they are ready to be tested, and mistakes are common.

It is better to provide exercises in which students can actually consolidate their learning. Instead of asking them to convert actives to passives, or past tenses to present, or infinitives to the correct tense, it is preferable to give the correct form, and require the students to make a correct choice without being distracted by the wrong form. For instance, if we want the students to practise matching the appropriate verb form with a singular or plural subject in the present simple tense, we can provide a series of sentences dealing with both singular and plural on the topic, for example *The horse/ horses is/are four legged animals/a four legged animal. They/it eats/eat grass*. The students' task is to write out a paragraph with either a singular or plural subject. Everything they need is provided, but what they have to do is to make a meaningful and systematic choice from the items given. They are not being required to carry out a conversion exercise or to add anything new.

Another technique is to provide a type of substitution table from which the students have to select combinations to make up a series of correct sentences. Here is a very brief example:

They	met	to town.
John	went	at a restaurant.
He	ate	Mary.

In exercises of this type, the students not only have to make up correct sentences, but they also have to put them into a sequence which will form a brief narrative. There are clues to sequence in the above example – *John* would normally come in the first sentence to tell us the name of the actor. *He*, which is backward pointing, refers to *John* in the first sentence and so would be the subject of the second sentence. *They*, which refers to both *John* and *Mary*, would logically come in the third sentence, and so on.

This type of exercise brings us to the writing of connected sentences rather than isolated ones. It also introduces us to paragraph writing. This is an important step for anyone who wants to learn to use writing as a form of communication. In teaching writing beyond sentence level, we need to begin with a model text. The model provides the students with an example of what to do. This is important, because even when learning to write in our native language, we often refer to models as guides to our own writing. (The term 'model' here refers to any piece of acceptable writing of the desired type. It doesn't mean something which is 'perfect'.)

You can use the model as a reading comprehension passage so that it will serve a dual purpose. In the first part of the lesson, you can ask the students to deal with content (for comprehension) and language and organization (for subsequent application in their own writing). Information from the model text can be transferred to a worksheet as part of reading comprehension work.

When they have completed the worksheet, the students can then use it as a cue sheet in order to reconstruct the original text. In other words, they attempt to rewrite the model, though possibly in a shortened or simplified form. Their version will retain many of the important features of the original, though changes are permissible and may in fact be encouraged. For instance, you may wish to add some vocabulary practice to the exercise and this could lead to changes in words or expression in the version which the students produce.

Rewriting completes the first main stage. This can be followed by a second stage of parallel writing. In parallel writing the students are given new information which they use to write a parallel composition, similar in style to the original model. The main change lies in the content of the parallel version rather than in structures or functions. For instance, if you were dealing with narrative, you could give the students new information – possibly in pictorial form – which would require them to use many of the same verbs as in the original model text, but in a different sequence.

The final stage, which might be done as a homework assignment, involves the students writing compositions of their own. They can then exchange compositions with a partner. Each member of the pair reads his or her partner's composition and uses the information to carry out an information transfer activity similar to the one which they performed in the first lesson. Since neither member of the pair knows in advance exactly what the other partner is writing about, there is a communicative element to this writing. Furthermore, by writing for each other and subsequently discussing each other's compositions, students will begin to develop a sense of writing for an audience as well as realizing the importance of being explicit and accurate in what they write.

Another aspect of writing which needs developing is the organization of ideas. The ways of organizing ideas in English prose may be rather different from the conventions in the students' own language, and at intermediate or advanced level, students sometimes have trouble with organization and logic rather than with grammar or vocabulary. It is partly a matter of style. In English, the writer of objective, referential prose stands at a distance from his subject, and adopts an impersonal attitude towards the topic and the reader. Informal references to personal experience as evidence are usually considered inappropriate to this type of writing, whereas in some cultures such personal anecdote is perfectly acceptable as a way of stating evidence.

Another dimension of the same problem lies in the organization of a series of statements to indicate logical relationships such as concession, hypothesis, inference, deduction, and so on. In academic writing in English it is common to put forward an entirely hypothetical argument which is usually, but not always, signalled by *if*. Everything within the argument is hypothetical, including statements of concession or contrast. Students unfamiliar with these conventions will need help, not only in using such signals of meaning as *however*, *although* and *whereas*, but also in understanding the meaning of such signals as part of the total text.

As with the writing work outlined earlier, it is probably best to begin with examples of the type of writing which you wish to teach. You can focus the students' attention on various aspects of the model text, particularly the organization of ideas and the ways in which these ideas are expressed. The students can then be given parallel writing in which they apply features of the model text to a similar piece of prose. The final stage involves them in writing an original text of their own, incorporating the organization and logical features which they have practised in the preceding lessons.

Other writing activities which can be introduced at intermediate and advanced level include adding information to an existing text, deleting information from within a text and placing it elsewhere in the same passage, changing the emphasis or viewpoint and changing the function of a text (for example rewriting a description of a process as a set of instructions). Each of these is an authentic task because they are the kinds of activity which we often perform, even in everyday writing. For instance, one may face the problem of how to write an informal note to a friend or colleague who has failed, yet again, to perform a promised favour. There are subtleties of attitude and emphasis in such a note which might well result in writing several versions before the writer is satisfied that he has produced a message which was neither too aggrieved nor too forgiving!

Adding, deleting and reorganizing information are familiar activities to anyone who has to write reports, prepare proposals, argue a case or persuade an audience. At more advanced levels, these are skills which need practice. They don't have to be done as solo activities. They can be carried out as group or class activities, in which you and the students discuss the most appropriate place to add information, the changes which such additions will require and so on.

28

An important problem at all levels is that of dealing with errors and corrections. Unlike speaking, writing is the one productive skill in which we have time to think about what we have produced or are going to produce. This means that we can think not only about content and our intentions and meanings, but also about the form of what we will write. Furthermore, we can correct and modify as we write. Even fluent writers in their native language will tend to correct, reorganize and polish both during and after writing a first draft. The students need to be encouraged to develop these habits of self correction. They also need to be given some guidelines. If they feel that they have to correct everything, they will become discouraged and anxious.

If you are focusing on particular language and functional points in a writing lesson, tell the students to check their own work for the same features before they hand it to you for marking. In this way they may only need to check two or three particular features and they can be systematic about it rather than overwhelmed by having to check for lots of different items. It is also more likely that they will actually identify and correct errors if there are only a few things to look out for.

Gradually, over a series of lessons, you can focus the students' attention on different aspects, ranging from such elementary features as article usage to subject-verb agreement to punctuation (for example all sentences must end with a full stop) to the appropriate use of logical connectors like *however*, *but* and *although*. Your own marking of compositions can also focus on the same features so that the students know what you are looking for. You can also adopt a marking code, indicating in the margin the type of error by using a symbol or letter, for example *V* for verb, *Ag* for subject-verb agreement, *A* for article and so on. The sign in the margin alerts the student to the presence of an error in the line concerned. His task is to find the actual error and to correct it. Such a code assumes, of course, some knowledge of grammar on the part of the students.

The correction of errors is particularly important, and is something which it is wise to insist upon. Once you establish a habit of error correction, the students will write out the correct form, which you can then check when they next hand in their composition work. If you keep a record of compositions written, you can add another column to your records for corrections completed. Whether you adopt a strict attitude towards the correction of errors is up to you, but you may find that students like to know that you are taking an interest in their work by insisting on error correction and checking the corrections once they are done.

There is no need for the teacher to be burdened by checking and correcting compositions. You can share the task by having students check and correct each other's work. This fits in well with the kind of pair work communicative writing described earlier. It doesn't absolve the teacher from checking and correcting, but it does spread the load and it involves students in the responsibility of marking.

To summarize, writing at all levels involves moving from a model to parallel writing to the final stage, in which students produce an original piece of writing based on their own ideas and content. As well as the skills of producing grammatically correct sentences, writing involves producing logically organized prose which is stylistically appropriate to the writer's purpose. It is difficult to focus simultaneously on all of these aspects, and we need to help students by dealing systematically with one feature at a time. Students can also help each other and the teacher by assuming some of the responsibility for checking and error correction. The importance of accurate and explicit writing will be more obvious to students if they write for each other, as they then have a real audience, and they will have to explain to each other the errors and ambiguities which they find in each other's compositions.

Vocabulary and meaning

Meaning can be taught by demonstration, definition, translation or by working out from context. Demonstration is only possible with words whose meaning can be conveyed by pointing to something, such as an object, or demonstrating, such as a verb of action. You need to be careful when using demonstration, as students may not necessarily understand the meaning you intend. It is usually wise to refer to several things rather than just one if you want to demonstrate the meaning of a noun or an adjective. So, for example, if you want to teach the meaning of *chair*, you would show pictures of several different types of chair or point to actual chairs, otherwise students might think that the word applied only to the specific type of chair which you pointed to.

Definition as a means of conveying meaning can be carried out either in the native language or in English. Once the students have acquired a basic vocabulary, it is a good idea to use English as the defining language, since defining is part of the skill of explaining. Also, if students are going to be mixing with native English speakers at all, they are more likely to receive definitions in English than in their own native language.

Translation is the easiest way of conveying meaning. Even simple words, however, don't always have direct translation equivalents in the native language. The precise equivalent may depend, for example, on context, or on the specific type of thing referred to. So the choice of translation may be difficult and may confuse rather than help the students.

Finally, there is the use of context to work out word meaning. Although this can be a time-consuming procedure, it is worth training students to develop a technique that they can use when they don't have a teacher, a dictionary or a bilingual speaker to help them. Train students to decide, first of all, what part of speech the unknown word is. For instance, if the word is preceded by *the* or *a*, then it will probably be a noun. Next, they should look at the word in relation to other parts of the sentence. If, for instance, the unknown word is a transitive verb, they need to look at the subject and object of the verb. This will give them some idea of who does what to whom. Also, if the unknown word is a verb, there may be an associated adverb which gives a clue to meaning. If the unknown word is a noun, there may be an accompanying adjective which helps.

Using such contextual clues may still not enable the students to work out the precise meaning, but they may be able to derive sufficient meaning for the task in hand. Students may have to be persuaded that they don't need to know the full meaning of every new word they encounter. Even native speakers of English tolerate not knowing the full meaning of unfamiliar or new vocabulary, and it isn't realistic to try to gain a full definition at the first exposure. New meanings or extensions of meaning come as a result of further exposure to the word in new and varied contexts.

When students meet new words, encourage them to use the new words in sentences of their own. This will help them to discover the way in which the word can or can't be used. You can provide them with sentences in which they can substitute the new word for words already known. To demonstrate the precise use of words, prepare sentences with multiple choices at those points where the new vocabulary item occurs. The rest of the sentence or paragraph provides the context which limits the choice from the range of available words.

One aspect of meaning is the relationship of a work to other terms in the same area of meaning. Some words are more general in meaning, for example *a building*, while others are more specific, for example *a house*, and others are more specific still, for example *a cottage*. Although these are all synonyms, they can't all be used in the same context. Learning meaning involves learning the difference between the general terms and the more specific ones, and when and how to use them. Exercises which help students to discriminate between the general and the specific, a class and instances of the class, are an essential part of vocabulary teaching.

It is a good idea to encourage students to make up their own word lists and dictionaries. Not everyone is interested in the same things. Students will read different books and will pick up different vocabulary items. Encourage them to keep a card index or a small, alphabetically arranged note book in which they can maintain a record of vocabulary for themselves. Their vocabulary list can contain definitions as well as instances of the word in context. As a personal vocabulary list, it is something which the student creates himself and thus will probably have more interest and appeal than lists which are provided by the teacher.

Testing

As a teacher you will want to know how well your students are progressing and how effective your teaching has been. The students, for their part, need to be reassured that they are making progress and they will want to be shown how best they can improve their performance. So you need to use tests – either published ones, or tests that you have devised yourself.

What makes a good test? You should only test what you have chosen to test. Students shouldn't lose marks for errors in features not under review. It is important, therefore, to decide what you want to test. Students will see it as a fair test if it relates to what they have been taught. The questions should represent a fair sample of what the student should know, and not just be a series of trick questions and exceptions or obscure rules and structures.

If the test results are going to be used as the basis for an important decision, such as selection for a course or for promotion to a higher grade, then the questions must be of such a form that anyone marking them would arrive at the same total score. If no such vital decision is involved, you may take the opportunity of using tests which are less controlled, allowing the students to be more creative. Markers will then tend to vary in their opinions of the marks that should be given for such performance. In the classroom, the teacher's grade will usually be good enough, but if the test is an important one, then creative work – both spoken and written – will need to be assessed by more than one marker and their grades added together to give a final score. Double marking like this also protects teachers from criticism by students or parents because the final score is a combination of marks from two different markers.

What makes a good language test? In addition to the points already mentioned, a language test should reflect what we know about language learning and language behaviour. Make sure that you test not only form but also meaning, not just structures but functions too. The actual phrasing of the test instructions in English may prove to be more difficult for the students than the things you are testing, so you may find it best to use the native language for the rubrics and instructions.

Perhaps the most difficult task the teacher has to face is getting clear in his own mind what he wants to test. Here the syllabus outline which the teacher devised himself, or was given to teach from, and the contents pages of the textbooks used will be helpful. It is essential to have a clear idea not only of what you want to test, but also of the relative importance of various items. The syllabus will give a guide here by indicating how much time should be given to each item, and tests should reflect this. Because tests are so closely bound up with teaching objectives and methods, it is most unwise for a teacher to use just any test that falls to hand. There are various commonly used testing procedures.

Multiple choice

Example: He accused me of _____ lies.
(a) speaking (b) saying (c) telling (d) talking

Here one feature alone is tested. The possible answers tell the students what part of the verb is required. All they have to do is to select the correct vocabulary item. This is a very common procedure. It is objective and quickly scored. We need to ask ourselves, however, just how important the feature is that is being tested for a student's command of English and how like real English the test item is.

Cloze tests

A passage is chosen by the tester. He then removes every fifth, sixth or seventh word and leaves a blank space in its place. The students are required to read and understand the gapped passage and to write in the missing words. These words will be both vocabulary items and items of grammar. There should be about fifty gaps in all. Some people insist on there being only one correct answer. Others will accept answers that seem appropriate in the context. This method has the advantage of dealing with a large piece of authentic language that has meaning for the students and is more clearly related to real-life language use.

Communicative items

Example (a): Ask a friend for these things and thank him or her:
a pencil, an eraser, a pencil-sharpener.

Example (b): Ask a stranger the way to the following places:
the railway station, the main post office, the bus station.
Thank him or her.

In (a) the students are making requests and in (b) they are enquiring for information. The language they use should be appropriate. For example, the language they use with a stranger should differ from that which they use with a friend. The scoring of the answers should take this into account. The actual structures that the students use may differ from student to student. The teacher then has to decide how he will score the various answers. This is an example of the more creative type of response that students can be called upon to make.

Organization and management

The language syllabus

A syllabus is a programme for teaching. It states both the aims and content of what you will teach, and it may also say something about the methods and textbooks which the teacher and students will follow. Traditionally, language syllabuses have been structurally organized. The syllabus consists of a list of structures and vocabulary, carefully graded and sequenced. (See the discussion on grading.)

Recently there has been a shift to functionally organized syllabuses. Instead of taking a list of structures as the basis for the syllabus, a list of functions (such as inviting, reporting and thanking) has been used. This does not mean that structures and vocabulary are forgotten. A comprehensive syllabus will include these as well as a list of functions.

Because the functional use of language is concerned with doing things, it is possible to state the aims of a functional syllabus as pieces of behaviour. In doing so, we focus on what the students will be able to do, and how well they will be able to do it. So, for instance, we could state as an objective that the student will be able to find information on the departure and arrival times of trains, using questions with *What* and *When*. Or we might state as a more general objective that the student will be able to control a conversation with a native speaker until he has extracted the meaning he wants.

In addition to stating aims, objectives and content, the syllabus tells the teacher how much time to give to the various items outlined in the programme. The teacher needs to know whether to spend an hour, a week or a month on various items, and the syllabus should give some guidance on this matter.

Many teachers follow an examination prescription as their syllabus, and they teach what is specified in the exam specification. Examination syllabuses do change, however, and today many public examinations include functional as well as grammatical items. This means that the content and methods of the teaching programme will have to change as well.

Probably the simplest way to make such changes is to use a new textbook. The textbook will normally have been written according to a carefully devised syllabus. Your task as a teacher is to compare a selection of textbooks with the requirements of your own syllabus. If your syllabus is functionally based, then it makes sense to choose a textbook which has a similar basis. If your syllabus places a lot of emphasis on using the language for speaking and listening, you will need to choose materials which are designed to develop these particular skills.

Finally, the syllabus is a guide to the examiner or tester. It is also a guide to the students. The teacher, the students and the examiner will all know what should have been learnt if all of them are following the same syllabus. When you are setting examinations or tests, you should refer to your syllabus as this will guide you in the things you should test for. The syllabus will also tell you how important items are so that you won't give too much attention in a test to items that are of low value in the total programme.

Lesson planning

Busy teachers can't usually plan their lessons in great detail. Even so, all teachers need to think about the way they organize their lessons and if you are beginning English teaching, you do need to spend some time developing the skill of lesson planning. Often the teacher will think of the plan in terms of the content, for example, the third unit of the textbook. A plan should consider more than content, however. In planning a lesson you need to think of:

1 What language and behaviour students will be able to perform by the end of the lesson.
2 How well they will be able to perform these things.
3 What activities they will do during the lesson.
4 How much time you will spend on each part of the lesson.
5 What materials and aids you will need.

Typically, a lesson of forty-five minutes will consist of three main stages:

1 Presenting new language, either in spoken or written form.
2 Practising the new language.
3 Using the new language for communication.

The presentation stage may take from ten to fifteen minutes. The practice stage will tend to occupy fifteen to twenty minutes. The communication or exploitation stage will occupy about ten to twenty minutes. There is nothing sacred about these timings, but they do indicate the rough proportion of parts of the lesson, with more time being spent on practice than on any other stage.

A lesson plan is a plan of action and interaction. You may make decisions about the content and organization of the lesson, but you will actually be putting your plan into effect in cooperation with a group of students so you need to look at the lesson from their point of view as well as your own. This means that you have to think about the pace and timing of the lesson, the variety of activities which you and the students will perform, and the way in which these activities will be managed and organized. You will also be wise to have contingency plans, in case things don't go as you have planned. The contingency plan may be something as simple as knowing an easier exercise elsewhere in the textbook if the one you are going to take proves too difficult. You also need to think about the instructions you will give the students and the questions that you will ask them. If neither is clear, your lesson will be in difficulties.

If you are going to use audio or visual aids, you need to think about how you are going to exploit them. How, and in what order, will you display a picture sequence? How will you use pictures to present some new vocabulary items? Once presented, will you leave pictures on display throughout the lesson, or will you remove them from view once they have been used? These are the kinds of questions which have to be answered when planning a lesson.

You will also need to think about organizing pair or group work, particularly if it involves the students using pictures or cue cards. There are suggestions on organizing pair work in the sections on speaking and classroom management. The procedures outlined there show the sort of thing which you need to think through as you plan your lesson. Don't leave planning pair and group work until you arrive in the classroom, otherwise the resulting confusion may deter you and your class from using such activities again.

As a lesson plan is for your own guidance, it should be in a form which you can easily understand and follow. A very detailed lesson plan will be hard to follow during the lesson. It is better to have simple headings which you can read at a glance. More detailed guidance can usually be found in the teacher's book for the textbook that you are using. You can also write notes in your own copy of the student's book.

It is a good idea to note in your lesson plan the exercise or point at which you ended so that you know where to start your next lesson. You also need to note any homework that you set and the date it is to be handed in. Such notes are especially important if you only see the students once or twice a week and if you are teaching several classes at once.

If you find that the students have difficulties with any activity or exercise, note this in your lesson plan or in the textbook so that you can avoid these difficulties next time you teach the same lesson or material. You may find, for instance, that the lesson assumes that the students have already covered certain other material. If this is so, you would need to prepare the ground for a future group of students if you were to use the same material again.

As your experience of new methods and materials develops, you will find less and less detail is needed in your lesson plan. Even so, you will always need to go through the exercises before the lesson, writing in answers or extra examples in your own copy of the textbook, and making sure that you know what you and the students are supposed to do. Even the best textbooks contain items which can confuse the students, and unless you go over the lesson beforehand, you can find yourself in a difficult position in class if an unexpected problem occurs.

Classroom management

There are many things which the teacher has to be responsible for in the classroom. Some of these responsibilities can be shared with the students. For instance, we have already seen that learners should become more responsible for correcting their own errors and for marking their own work. You shouldn't, of course, hand over these responsibilities all at once. The sharing of responsibilities is a gradual process developed over many weeks or months.

At first the teacher has to establish conventions in the classroom. One of these can be that everyone must speak English as much as possible. There will be occasions, though, when the native language may be more efficient and effective, as when giving explanations and complicated instructions. Such instructions may be required when you are training the students in pair and group work.

Teachers are sometimes afraid of pair and group work because they fear that both they and the class will be confused. It is a good idea always to demonstrate to the class what you want them to do. This may mean treating them as one half of the pair as a first stage of preparing them for pair work as described in the section on speaking. After you have done some teacher-class pair work, bring two students to the front of the class and get them to carry out a pair work demonstration. This will show the class exactly what they should do.

In pair work, make sure that the members of the pair face each other. This can be difficult if the chairs and desks all face the front of the room. Tell the students to shift their chairs so that they face each other. They don't usually have to shift their desks in order to do this. Another way is to tell alternate rows to turn round and face the row behind them. This means that for a class sitting in four rows, you will have two sets of rows facing each other. In group work, you can use a variation on this procedure. Alternate rows turn round to face the row behind them, and then two adjacent pairs form groups of four. If you require larger groups than this, three groups of adjacent pairs can form a group of six. Six is generally the maximum useful size for group work. If you want to shift people around from group to group in order to exchange information, tell the students in each group to number off from one to four, five or six, depending on the size of the groups. Then, when the groups are to exchange information, all the 'ones' come together, all the 'twos' come together, and so on. In this way, new groups will be formed, made up of a member of each of the previous groups.

You can avoid a lot of furniture shifting and noise if you arrange the classroom so that there are groups of four students facing each other around a table. They can easily turn their chairs to face the front of the class when you are using the board or other visual aids.

Grouping students can be useful if you are teaching a multiple-ability class, in which the students aren't streamed according to their linguistic level or ability. It is difficult to teach such classes as a uniform group, so putting them into sub-groups is helpful. It is also a good idea to have some different or extra work ready for the major ability levels within the class and it is obviously easier to distribute the material if the members of each level are grouped together. You can also ask the quicker or more advanced students to help the slower students, and this is more easily done if the students are organized into smaller groups according to level. Members of the more advanced group can join other groups when appropriate during the lesson, and subsequently return to their own group.

Splitting a very large class into sub-groups is also possible. In fact, group and pair work will normally occupy only part of a class period, so you do not need to worry about having a large class of fifty or so students making a lot of noise throughout the period. Once you establish the organization of such group work, the class should quickly form sub-groups and will get on with the group work quietly and efficiently. Noise is likely to occur when they don't know what to do and are confused. Clear instructions and demonstration will help to avoid such confusion and noise.

Even when the students are performing pair and group work, the teacher still has a role to play. You will find it necessary to circulate unobtrusively around the room, listening to the students, noting difficulties or errors, and helping where necessary. If there is general difficulty or confusion, intervene by stopping the class and going back over the problem area. If, however, the work is proceeding smoothly, don't interfere. Your achievement as a teacher lies in bringing your students to the point where they can carry out such activities independently.

Grammar

There is no general agreement on the place of grammar in language teaching. Audio-lingualism avoids stating grammatical rules, whereas some structurally based courses make explicit grammatical statements. Some approaches prefer to give grammatical rules to the students, whereas others prefer to have the students work out the rules for themselves. As in all areas of language teaching, it is unwise to be dogmatic about the place of grammar, and it seems sensible to make use of explicit grammatical rules as summaries of the way the language is organized.

The place of grammatical rules and terminology in your teaching will depend on the age of the students. There is very little point in making use of such rules with children, for whom abstract rules of grammar will make little sense. Older learners, and particularly adults, will often prefer to use such rules and they will be more able to understand them. You need to distinguish, however, between the learning of a rule and actually applying the rule when using the language. It is one thing to know that there is a class of verbs rarely used in the present continuous (e.g. *have, like, see, hear*), but another thing to apply this knowledge when speaking English. The rule will only become part of the students' competence if they have lots of practice in which the rule is applied.

Rather than learning grammatical rules, students are more likely to benefit if they are helped to see patterns and regularities in the language. For instance, the regular countable nouns in English form the plural by the addition of -*s*. Regular verbs form the past tense by the addition of -*ed*. Nouns occur either at the beginning of a sentence or after the verb. These are regularities or patterns which students should be helped to see . Without gaining some understanding of such patterns, the students won't be able to make up new sentences of their own.

It is helpful if students can see a connection between grammatical forms and the functional use of language. For example, the interrogative form with *did* is typically associated with asking for information. A sequence of statements containing past tense verbs is typically linked with the function of narrating. There are many other typical associations of language form and function, and students will benefit from forming such associations. When you then want to introduce them to variations, such as the use of the interrogative to express surprise, they have a standard or basis for comparison. Stylistically unusual or expressive uses of language only make sense if the general or typical is already known, and it is here that the teaching of grammar may have a useful place.

Finally, as we noted in the discussion on correcting errors in writing and on the use of context when working out the meaning of vocabulary, a knowledge of grammar and grammatical terminology may be useful for the students. The teaching of some grammar may be essential as a way of helping the learning of vocabulary and the skill of writing. Indeed, it is difficult to see how to avoid explicit reference to grammar when teaching writing beyond the most elementary type of copying or transformation exercises. The choice of terminology is up to the teacher. The important thing is to be consistent and to use a widely recognized set of terms. A good rule is to use the same terminology that is used in the students' textbook, since our aim is to enlighten rather than confuse the students.

Audio-visual aids

The blackboard or whiteboard

The blackboard is your most important visual aid. Most classrooms have either a blackboard and chalk, or a whiteboard and a felt-tip pen. The board can be used for presenting drawings, diagrams and language. It is important to develop skill and technique in using the board.

Plan how you are going to use your board. It is a good idea to divide it into two sections. In one section you can put material that you want to keep for reference throughout the lesson. Use the other section for temporary material which you rub out and replace during the course of the lesson. This is your working half of the board.

If you aren't familiar with using the board, practise printing words and sentences on it. Go to the rear of the classroom to see how easy to read your printing is. Do the same for drawings, diagrams and tables. Obtaining a 'students' eye view' will help you to develop your technique.

Here are some ways to use the board. Write new and unfamiliar words on the board as you introduce them in a lesson. Build up dialogues and paragraphs on the board by eliciting language from the students. Put an incomplete text on the board and ask the class to suggest completions. Use the board as a worksheet for listening and reading comprehension, particularly if you don't have paper-copying facilities, and then ask the class to copy it into their exercise books. After they have completed their own individual worksheets, use your blackboard version for checking the completed version.

As well as putting things on the board, you can also wipe things off. For instance, if you build up a text or a dialogue on the board, you can rub out parts of the text and ask the class to complete the text from memory. The task will become more challenging, and often very amusing, as you rub out more and more and the students have to produce more and more of the text. The board is a very effective device for using this technique of the 'disappearing text'.

Good boardmanship begins when you enter the classroom. Always clean the board before you begin teaching because existing material on the board can be distracting and confusing. If necessary, carry some chalk or a felt-tip pen with you. At the end of the lesson, clean the board for the next teacher.

Visual aids

As well as the board, you can use visual aids such as magazine pictures and wall charts. It is a good idea to build up a magazine picture library, using illustrations from colour magazines, brochures and catalogues. Cut the pictures out, omitting any irrelevant material such as captions and slogans.

Paste them onto thin cardboard so that they are easy to handle and preserve. Make notes on the back about how you used them. The notes can be very brief, and may refer to structures or functions or topics for which the picture is useful. Then file the pictures according to their teaching function.

If you or one of your colleagues is a good artist, you can make your own wall pictures to illustrate scenes, situations and objects. Alternatively, you can buy commercially prepared picture sets, which can be used for picture compositions or as prompts for spoken practice. Wall charts shouldn't contain too much detail. Some of the original wall picture sets are so full of detail that they are confusing both for the student and the teacher.

Pictures are useful substitutes for real objects. When you are teaching vocabulary for items like food, clothing, domestic appliances and various everyday objects, it is more convenient to have pictures rather than the objects themselves. If you have multiple sets of such pictures, they can be used for pair or group work, especially for dialogue practice. Commercially produced picture sets of objects with suggestions for dialogue and pair work are available.

Don't use the same picture or pictures over and over again for different purposes. Quite apart from boring the students, it will be confusing for them if they have to associate quite different language with one and the same picture. Each picture is usually more appropriate for some purposes than others. For instance, if you are teaching students to describe things, people or places, a single picture will be sufficient. If, however, you are teaching anything which involves the idea of sequence, a series of pictures will be needed. It is very difficult to teach story-telling using just one picture because normally a story involves a series of events or happenings.

Audio aids

The cassette recorder has been a very welcome addition to teaching materials. Cassettes are much easier to use than open-reel tapes, and you can even make your own material using a recorder with a built-in microphone. You can also take recordings off the radio to provide authentic material for listening practice.

Familiarize yourself with the recorder and learn how to manipulate the buttons or keys. Do this in the privacy of an empty classroom. Remember to put the counter to zero when you insert a cassette, and note, too, the counter number of sections that you wish to return to. If you are working from a unit in the middle of the tape, you can set the counter to zero at the beginning of the section you want to use. This makes it easier when you want to replay the same piece of material during the lesson.

Try various combinations of the sound controls in order to find the most audible combination for your classroom. It is generally unwise to turn the volume up as far as possible, because there is too much distortion. You may find it better to use the tone control to improve audibility.

Using a dictionary

The suggestions which follow relate to the *Easy English Dictionary*, published by Harrap. You will be able to adapt these suggestions to whatever dictionary you are using. First of all, familiarize your students with the contents and organization of the dictionary. Review the main sections, beginning with the phonetic symbols and abbreviations. Then run over the sections at the back of the dictionary. Finally, deal with some definitions so that the students will become familiar with the lay-out and conventions which are followed in the dictionary entries. Note, for instance, that the past tense form of a verb is always given as part of a short sentence. Make sure students understand the meaning of abbreviations like *v.*, *adv.* and so on as used in the entries, and refer them to the key in the front of the dictionary.

Once students have been shown the main sections of the dictionary, give them some exercises which will require them to search for definitions and information, or use the companion workbook, *Making the most of your Easy English Dictionary*, published by Harrap. The exercises should cover three main sections: Definitions, Grammar and Useful Information. Spread the exercises over several lessons rather than trying to deal with everything at once.

When dealing with definitions, it is important to give words in a sentence context. For instance, a word like *tug* changes its part of speech and its meaning, depending on whether it is used as a noun or a verb. Even as a noun, it can mean a sharp pull or a powerful boat used to tow other boats. Instead of asking students simply to look up words in a vocabulary list, give them words in sentence contexts, so they have to identify the part of speech of the word from the context before they look it up in the dictionary. The entry in the dictionary will give them plenty of help in finding the correct part of speech and the meaning. All words are shown in a phrase or sentence. Students can then make up other sentences using the model in the dictionary entry.

In addition to dealing with meaning and use in sentences, set students the task of finding out the pronunciation of selected words. This will require some work on the phonetic symbols and their relationship to English sounds. You should also ask students to look up the stress for various words. For example, is *protest* (verb) stressed on the first or second syllable?

The grammar section will consolidate rules which either you or the textbook provide. You can refer students to the relevant part of the grammar section when dealing with particular points. This section can become the students' own reference grammar which they can use when working at home or without a teacher. Encourage them to make use of the grammar notes by setting the occasional exercise which will require reference to parts of this section, such as those dealing with the rules for forming plural nouns, prepositions and phrasal verbs.

You can use the Useful Information section for quizzes. Students can make up questions based on the information given in this section. Alternatively, you can set them quizzes, the answers to which must be found in this section.

Finally, encourage the students to use the dictionary as a tool. They should always have it to hand and should consult the dictionary before coming to you for help. Remind your students that they can always carry the dictionary with them, but they can't always have you by their side. Their dictionary will be a useful and informative companion.

Further reading

What follows is a short and very selective list of titles for further reading. Where possible, the titles selected are of a practical, classroom based character, and they are representative of good current practice. A list of journals and magazines is also included.

The list does not provide any suggestions for actual teaching materials. There is now such an extensive selection of ELT materials that even a short list would be beyond the scope of this publication. However, a very useful survey of ELT materials is published by English Language Teaching Information Services (ELTIS), 66 York Road, Weybridge, Surrey KT13 9ET, England.

Journals and magazines

English Language Teaching Journal (*ELTJ*) Quarterly Journals Department, Oxford University Press, Walton Street, Oxford OX2 6DP, England.

Modern English Teacher (*MET*) Quarterly MEP, PO Box 129, Oxford OX2 8JU, England.

Practical English Teaching (*PET*) Quarterly Brookhampton Lane, Kineton, Warwick CV35 0JB, England.

World Language English Quarterly Pergamon Press, Headington Hill Hall, Oxford OX3 0BW, England.

MET and PET are particularly good sources of useful classroom techniques and ideas.

General methodology

Abbott, G and Wingard, P (eds) *The Teaching of English as an International Language*. London, Collins (1981).

Broughton, G, Brumfit, C, et al *Teaching English as a Foreign Language*. London, Routledge (1978).

Rivers, W and Temperley, M *A Practical Guide to the Teaching of English*. London, Oxford University Press (2nd edition, 1981).

Communicative methodology

Johnson, K and Morrow, K (eds) *Communication in the Classroom*. London, Longman (1981).

Littlewood, W *Communicative Language Teaching*. Cambridge, Cambridge University Press (1981).

Listening

Field, J *Listening Comprehension*. London, Macmillan (1981).
Maley, A L 'The Teaching of Listening Comprehension Skills' in *Modern English Teacher*, vol 6, no 3, pp 6–9 (1978).
Porter, D and Roberts, J 'Authentic Listening Activities' in *English Language Teaching Journal*, vol 36/1, pp 37–47 (1981).

Reading

Grellet, F *Developing Reading Skills*. Cambridge, Cambridge University Press (1981).
Nuttall, C *Teaching Reading Skills in a Foreign Language*. London, Heinemann (1982).
Williams, E *Reading Comprehension Techniques in English*. London, Macmillan (1982).

Speaking

Byrne, D *Teaching Oral English*. London, Longman (1976).
Revell, J *Teaching Techniques for Communicative English*. London, Macmillan (1980).
Ur, P *Discussions That Work*. Cambridge, Cambridge University Press (1982).

Writing

Byrne, D *Teaching Writing Skills*. London, Longman (1979).
Hodlin, S and Hodlin, T *Writing Letters in English*. London, Oxford University Press (1979).
White, R V *Teaching Written English*. London, Heinemann (1980).

Testing

Heaton, J B *Writing English Language Tests*. London, Longman (1975).
Heaton, J B (ed) *Language Testing*. Modern English Publications (1982).

Vocabulary Teaching

Tomlinson, B *Teaching Vocabulary*. London, Macmillan (1981).
Wallace, M *Teaching Vocabulary*. London, Heinemann (1982).

Drama techniques

Holden, S *Drama in Language Teaching.* London, Longman (1982).
Maley, A and Duff, A *Drama Techniques in Language Learning.* Cambridge, Cambridge University Press (New edition 1982).

The visual element

Ayton, A and Morgan, M *Photographic Slides in Language Teaching.* London, Heinemann (1981).
Byrne, D *Using the Magnetboard.* London, Heinemann (1980).
Holden, S (ed) *Visual Aids for Classroom Interaction.* Modern English Publications (1978).
Jones, J R H *Using the Overhead Projector.* London, Heinemann (1982).
McAlpin, J *The Magazine Picture Library.* London, Heinemann (1980).
Mugglestone, P *Planning and Using the Blackboard.* London, Heinemann (1980).
Shaw, P and de Vet, T *Using Blackboard Drawing.* London, Heinemann (1980).
Wright, A *Visual Materials for the Language Teacher.* London, Longman (1976).

Grammar and language

Bolitho, R and Tomlinson, B *Discover English.* London, Heinemann (1980).
Heaton, B *Using English in the Classroom.* London, Longman (1981).
Quirk, R and Greenbaum, S *A University Grammar of English.* London, Longman (1973).
Swan, M *Practical English Usage.* London, Oxford University Press (1980).
Wills, J *Teaching English Through English.* London, Longman (1981).
Winter, M *Harrap's Pocket English Grammar.* London, Harrap (1981).